CW00323646

Pergamano®

Parchment Craft

Over 15 original projects plus dozens of new design ideas

MARTHA OSPINA

NEW HOLLAND

To Cecile, Randi and Chikako

First published in 1998 by
New Holland Publishers (UK) Ltd
London • Cape Town • Sydney • Singapore

24 Nutford Place
London W1H 6DQ
United Kingdom

80 McKenzie Street
Cape Town 8001
South Africa

3/2 Aquatic Drive
Frenchs Forest, NSW 2086
Australia

ISBN 1 85368 820 7 (hb)
ISBN 1 85974 082 0 (pb)

Designer: Peter Crump
Editor: Gillian Haslam
Photographer: Shona Wood

Managing Editor: Coral Walker

2 4 6 8 10 9 7 5 3 1

Reproduction by PICA Colour Separation, Singapore
Printed and bound in Malaysia by Times Offset (M) sdn. Bhd

Contents

Introduction

I was delighted to be asked to write this book about parchment craft as it is my hobby, my fascination and my addiction. I first learnt this craft as a 14-year-old schoolgirl in Colombia in South America. I enjoyed it from the very beginning and started to make celebration cards for my parents and for my friends. People soon began to place orders with me, sometimes for as many as 100 invitation cards for a confirmation or a wedding. My reputation spread and soon I was asked to teach the craft to others. It was nice to see how my hobby became my work.

Despite my enjoyment in teaching, I had an overwhelming dream – to see Europe! A girlfriend and I saved hard for the trip until one day we boarded the plane and left for Europe. This trip was to change my entire life as I met a Dutchman, fell in love and came to live in the Netherlands.

I wanted to learn the Dutch language and to meet the people in my new country, so I joined a flower-arranging course. I showed my parchment cards to some of my fellow students. They were amazed at the beauty of the pieces and asked me to teach them the skills.

As the popularity of this craft grew, I started to instruct teachers both in the Netherlands and abroad. My husband and I started a parchment craft foundation and published a magazine about the craft.

So what exactly is parchment craft? It involves using parchment paper; a strong and flexible translucent paper. The techniques used include tracing from a design, embossing (raising) the pattern, perforating, cutting, painting and creative art stamping. You can make beautiful greetings and celebration cards, decorated envelopes, splendid wall decorations, colourful bookmarks, lampshades and cut-out cards with stained glass effects. It is also possible to make your work three-dimensional and produce delicate gift boxes, lovely baby booties and even very realistic flowers. The lacy borders made by perforations and cuttings are gorgeous and are the hallmark of the craft. If you see them you would not believe they are made from parchment paper.

This book is aimed at both newcomers to this craft and more experienced craftspeople. To help beginners, the book is divided into different projects, each one teaching you a new technique and enabling you to build up a repertoire of skills. You will need to start with the first project and gradually work your way through the book. When you reach the final project, you will have mastered all the different techniques of parchment craft. The techniques may look slightly complicated, but don't be alarmed. They really are easy to master. For the more experienced, this book is a source of new patterns and ideas.

I hope you enjoy your parchment craft!

Martha Ospina

THE HISTORY OF PARCHMENT CRAFT

Until the advent of papermaking (China in AD200 and much later – the twelfth century – in Europe) man wrote on papyrus made from dried plant leaves, and later, parchment.

Like many things born of necessity, parchment was invented in the Turkish city of Bergama (Pergamum in Latin) when people were forced to look for an alternative to papyrus as local wars prevented the importation of its raw materials. They found that specially prepared pig and antelope skin was the perfect solution to their papyrus shortage. This new material was named particaminum (from which we derive the word "parchment") partly after the city where it was discovered and also from the Latin *Pathica pellis* (Parthian skin).

During the fourteenth and fifteenth centuries, parchment was gradually replaced by paper in Europe as papermaking became more widespread. However, parchment was still highly valued and was used for books and important documents. Until the sixteenth century, parchment books were all hand-written – an extremely lengthy task carried out to the highest standards by monks and nuns. These books were highly colourful, and featured illuminated characters (the opening letter of a chapter which was decorated in gold and jewel-like colours). Wall decorations were also made from parchment. These were mainly religious pictures featuring Christ on the cross and images of saints.

The invention of the printing press in the fifteenth century changed this industry forever. Parchment was then used just for small devotional pictures, popular in religious circles. As demand for these pictures grew, parchment was replaced by paper.

In the sixteenth century, Columbus travelled to South America and early European settlers brought various skills with them, including the craft of working with parchment. The South American people, devoted to their religion and also known for their dexterity with their hands, started to make religious pictures with parchment, and later with parchment paper.

This craft, which started in Europe and then travelled to South America, is now enjoying huge popularity worldwide. Modern-day parchment paper is not made from skin, but is wood-based like any other type of paper. It is specially treated to give it its fine texture and appearance.

The scope of parchment craft has broadened from being used purely for religious works of art to encompass all manner of articles, from greetings cards to wall decorations, bookmarks, lampshades and flowers. All these are represented in the projects in this book. However, when you have worked your way through to the final project, you will find that the stunning medieval-style picture brings us back to the origins of parchment craft.

Early pieces of parchment craft usually depicted religious subjects and contained verses from the Bible.

How to use this book

This book is for beginners as well as advanced parchment crafters. The advanced ones amongst us might already know the majority of the techniques, but I am sure you will find valuable additional information and many patterns and ideas to copy and adapt.

If you are a beginner, do not be alarmed by all the techniques – this book does contain a lot of explanation and general information. All you need to do is start at the beginning with the first project and follow the order of the book. Always read through the entire project before you start to make the item.

The first project concentrates on teaching two simple techniques, so try to master those before moving on to the next project. Practise on a scrap of paper first – the techniques all become easier the more you practise.

After you have made all 16 projects, you will be able to master any parchment craft project – you could try those on the gallery pages.

Parchment craft does not cause a mess and you do not require a lot of space. You simply need a table, a good chair and, most importantly, very good light. This is delicate and fine work so you need this for good results and to avoid straining your eyes.

BASIC TECHNIQUES

To look at, parchment paper is similar to tracing paper. Its thickness, translucence and flexibility is quite different, however, and allows you to use a wide variety of techniques, including cutting, embossing and colouring. These will transform the original parchment paper into a different-looking material all together. And each technique can be used to create a really wide array of designs and patterns. I can assure you that you will never become bored with this craft!

Each project teaches a different technique, illustrated in detail with step-by-step photographs, so what is shown here is simply a summary of the varied skills you will learn. For those with some knowledge of parchment craft, you will find all the techniques, neatly catalogued in this book, of great use as a reference, and a help if you have had trouble mastering anything in particular.

So have fun, and remember – practice makes perfect!

Tracing (project 1)
Tracing involves copying the outlines of a pattern using ink and a mapping pen. The translucent parchment paper is laid on top of the pattern (patterns for all the projects are provided at the back of the book). White or coloured inks are used, depending on whether the outlines are to be seen in the finished piece.

When perforating the parchment paper, you pierce right through to the pattern. To avoid damaging your book, first make a photocopy of the pattern (you will not infringe the copyright if you make copies for your personal use).

Embossing (project 1)
Embossing means raising parts of the design by rubbing the surface with a metal tool. The paper fibres are stretched and compressed by the pressure of the tool and the natural light grey colour of the parchment paper will change to satin white. Applying soft pressure results in a half tone of white; higher pressure produces a proper white tone. By changing the intensity of the embossing you can achieve a mixture of tones, thus allowing you to make beautiful pictures by using just one single technique.

Perforating (projects 2, 5, 10 and 11)
Here, parchment paper is pierced with a tool with needles set into its tip. There are several perforating tools, each with a different number of needles. These needles are sharp, so take care. The perforations are often made along borders and the piercing is done either with the pattern underneath or over a special metal grid. The dots on the patterns or the openings in the metal grid show where to perforate.

Stippling (project 2)
This very pretty effect is produced with the single needle perforating tool. Many tiny perforations are made at random, very close together. The result is a soft white surface on the parchment paper. To achieve a more even and regular stippled result, place the parchment paper onto a piece of hard cardboard before you begin perforating.

Cutting and lace work (projects 2, 5 and 16)
Undoubtedly, the hallmark of parchment craft is the exquisite lacy designs which form patterns and borders. To achieve this effect, you must cut the perforations to form crosses, slits or other decorative shapes. A contrasting background for your project will emphasise the pattern. You will see in project 16 that tiny petals, leaves, stars and so on are often embossed in the spaces between the lacework. The variation of patterns is endless.

Painting (projects 6, 9 and 12)
Painting is an important technique. In parchment craft, the painting is limited to applying colours within the traced outlines of the designs. This makes painting simple and brings it within the reach of everyone, even those who did not think themselves capable of painting with a paintbrush and art paint. Here we use Tinta inks, Pintura paints, Pinta-Perla paints, Perga-Color felt tip pens and Perga-Liners colour pencils.

Dorsing (project 3)
Dorsing means changing the colour of the parchment paper from its original light grey to other soft colours using special Dorso crayons. An entire sheet or just a part of it, i.e. the blue for sky or water and green for meadows, etc., can be dorsed. The colour is applied to the reverse of the paper and not directly on top. Dorso crayons come in a wide range of colours.

Stamping (projects 6 and 7)
A different way of applying a design to parchment paper is by using a creative stamp. Pergamano stamps have an open line structure, so choose these rather than stamps which have a tighter design, as the latter will allow the paint to spread and to stain. Parchment paper does not absorb the dye quickly, so do allow it time to dry. Stamped designs can be embossed with silver embossing powder or painted with transparent colours. When displayed against light, these pieces resemble stained glass.

Materials & Equipment

The projects in this book all use Pergamano materials. See page 79 for stockists. The range of Pergamano materials includes:

Parchment paper: this 150 gsm paper is usually pale grey in colour, but can be red, blue, white or even rainbow.

Mapping pen: a tracing pen with a fine nib.

Embossing tools: there is a range of these, including fine stylus, extra fine, small and large ball and a hockeystick shaped tool.

Embossing pads: these include a small blue pad, "De Luxe" and "King-Size" black pads.

Perforating tools: these include 1-, 2-, 3-, 4- and 5-needle tools, a 7-needle or flower tool and a semi-circle tool.

"Excellent" perforating pad: a black synthetic pad on which to perforate your patterns.

Pergamano scissors: special scissors with curved blades for cutting perforations.

Dorso crayons: assortment 1 contains violet, magenta, blue, yellow ochre, skin colour, yellow, light green and turquoise. Assortment 2 contains light blue, red, brown, orange, lilac, green, light brown and black.

Tinta inks: available in 15 ml glass pots. White 01T, blue 02T, red 03T, green 04T, turquoise 05T, violet 07T, leaf green 10T, black 11T, sepia 12T, yellow 16T, fuchsia 20T, silver 21T and gold 22T.

Pintura paints: acrylic paints with a glossy appearance in 22 ml plastic dispensers. White 01, blue 02, red 03, light green 04, yellow ochre 05, orange 06, violet 07, green 08, black 11, brown 12, skin 13, yellow 16, fuchsia 20, grey 34, turquoise 48, bordeaux 51 and cinnamon 52.

Pinta-Perla paints: mother-of-pearl paints in 22 ml pots. White 01N, blue 02N, red 03N, light green 04N, violet 07N, green 08N, brown 12N, skin 13N, yellow 16N, fuchsia 20N, bronze 30N.

Perga-Colors: a set of 12 special felt tip pens.

Perga-Liners: soft matt colour pencils. Type A pencils are water-based, Type B oil-based. The Perga-Liner Combi Box 1 contains 20 short type A pencils and 11 long type B pencils. Box 2 contains 20 long type A pencils. The Duo Pencil Sharpener can be used for both types of pencil.

"Easy-Grid" Perforating Template: for use in the Brazilian perforating technique with the "Diamond" perforating tool.

Pergamano stamps: flowers in tiffany PS1, tropical bird PS2, Christmas crystal PS3, four hearts PS4, Art Nouveau tulips PS5, creative tulip PS6. Used with the Pergamano stamping ruler.

Brushes: Pergamano paintbrushes no. 0 and no. 2, Kolinsky paintbrush no. 2, special paintbrush no. 2 for use with the range of Perga-Color pens.

Miscellaneous: eraser for Tinta inks, Perga-Soft for embossing and perforating tools, Pergakit viscous glue, Pergamano sponge.

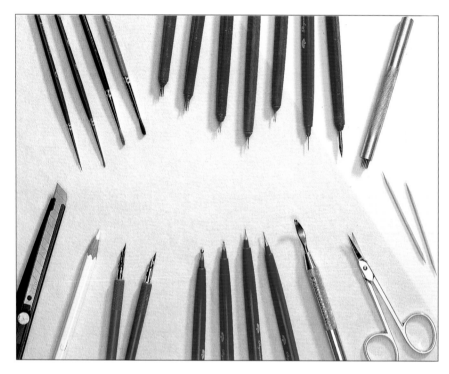

Projects and Galleries

Here's where the fun starts! For those experienced at parchment craft, you will be eager to turn the pages and see 16 completely new, step-by-step projects. For those starting out, begin with the first project – the Water Lily Card – and you will soon develop the skills required to progress to the second, third and fourth designs. By then you should be hooked!

The five galleries interspersing the projects display a beautiful array of different items: from greetings cards to lampshades, wedding bouquets to placemats, and each gallery is proof positive of the wonderful versatility of this exquisite craft. For those keen to make some of the delightful gifts shown in the galleries, you will be pleased to know that patterns appear for every item you see.

Tracing and embossing
WATER LILY CARD

Parchment craft is within the reach of everyone. You do not even need to be a designer as all the patterns are provided. This simple project uses only the techniques of tracing and embossing, enabling you to make your first beautiful piece without any difficulty!

You will need

*Parchment paper, size A4
(215 x 290 mm / 8½ x 11½ in)*

Adhesive tape

Patterns (see page 70)

Tinta ink: white 01T

Mapping pen

Water

Kitchen paper

White pencil

Embossing tools – all types

Embossing pad

Perga-Soft

Thick cardboard

Ruler

Craft knife

Before you trace the patterns on page 70, make a photocopy of them. There is an embossing practise sheet to help you. Place a sheet of parchment paper over this pattern. You will see different lines and shapes from the project with tool information. Use this exercise sheet for practising tracing and embossing. The project is a folding card and the overlap at the dashed line side must be at least the size shown on the pattern. Fix the parchment over the pattern with adhesive tape. You are now ready to begin.

1 Shake the bottle of Tinta white ink well. Dip the nib of the mapping pen into the ink as far as the small hole, then shake off the surplus ink by tapping the nib on the rim of the bottle. Trace over all the lines on the pattern. Try to make fine lines; after the embossing steps the outlines should be almost invisible. Hold the pen rather upright and do not press on the pen, let it glide. Always start your pen on a piece of scrap paper. At intervals, clean the pen in water, dry it and then continue. Folding lines should be marked with a white pencil.

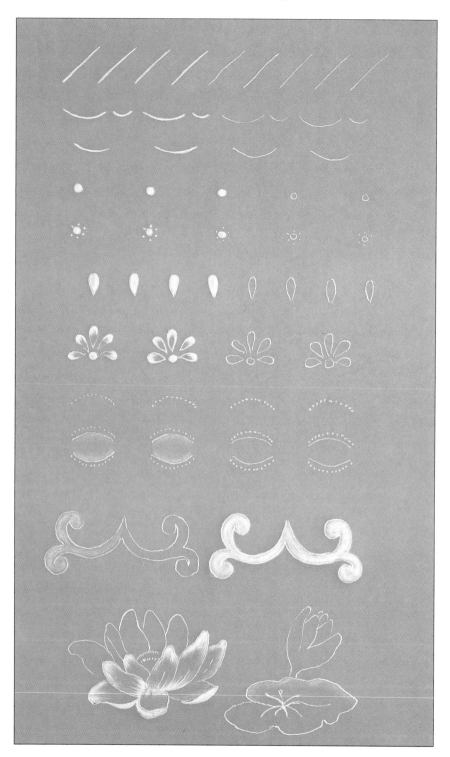

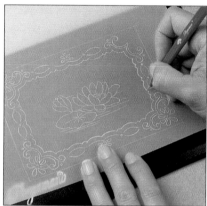

2 Next, emboss the lines with a fine stylus. Separate the parchment paper from the pattern and place the paper face down on the embossing pad. Dip the top of the fine stylus into the Perga-Soft first to aid its movement on the paper. Holding the fine stylus upright, draw over the paper, applying a little pressure. Try to follow the white ink line precisely.

These are the various patterns used for the Water lily card. They are created by embossing: a technique that is not difficult, but just takes a little practise to get right. Make sure you are comfortable holding your embossing tool. By varying the pressure, you will achieve different results. A firm, but gentle, pressure will result in a bright, white finish. A softer touch will produce a more subtle result.

3 To emboss the dots, use the extra fine ball tool. Rub the ball of the tool lightly over the Perga-Soft. First move the ball up and down on the paper, applying a little pressure initially. After the dot becomes white, increase the pressure. Finish the dot with a circular movement along the inside of the circles.

4 Emboss the teardrop shapes with the extra fine ball tool. Move the tool up and down in the direction of the shape. Start with a fairly light pressure and increase the pressure slowly. To complete the embossing, work precisely along the traced outlines: this will hide the white pen lines and give a neat finish.

5 Emboss the ornaments with the large ball tool. Move the tool in the direction of the shape, making long, smooth strokes. Do not press too hard and take your time. After the paper turns to white you can gradually increase the pressure.

6 Emboss the leaves with the hockey stick tool. To achieve the shadow effects, point the tip of the tool towards the outline of the leaves. Turn the paper while working along the outlines of the leaves. Put the pressure at the tip of the tool so the embossing fades towards the centre of the leaf. You may need to practise to find the correct angle of the tool for this effect.

7 To ensure your card folds neatly without cracking or splitting, emboss the folding line on the reverse side with the small ball tool, using a ruler. Fold the card and gently flatten the fold. A sharp fold will weaken the paper, so take care when you do this.

8 Place the completed card onto a cutting mat or thick piece of cardboard. Using a sharp craft knife and a ruler, carefully trim the card to size. Slip a piece of pink paper inside the card.

TIPS

• A new nib is often greasy, which prevents the ink from flowing down. Clean the nib with a drop of diluted washing up liquid and dry it with cotton rag.

• Always use a piece of cardboard to protect your table.

• When embossing tiny spots like dots, you can use the reverse side of the embossing pad. You will need more force, but the risk of damaging the parchment paper is less.

• To prevent the parchment paper becoming greasy or dirty from your hands, place a piece of scrap paper below your hand as you work.

• Slip a piece of folded, dark-coloured paper inside embossed white cards to emphasise their beauty.

Tracing with gold, stippling, perforating and cutting

GIFT BAG

Gold ink looks beautiful on parchment, so it is worth learning how to work with it. The stippling results in fine perforations, changing the parchment from light grey to a matt greyish-white. Perforated borders give a delicate, artistic finish to this delicate bag.

You will need

Parchment paper, size A4 (215 x 290 mm / 8½ x 11½ in)	Pergamano eraser or razor blade
Pattern (see page 70)	1- and 2-needle perforating tools
Adhesive tape	Perforating pad
Mapping pen	Small and large ball embossing tools
Tinta ink: gold 22T	Embossing pad
Cocktail stick or wooden skewer	Perga-Soft
Water	Pergamano scissors
Cotton rag	Ruler
Kitchen paper	Craft knife

Tinta gold and silver inks are different from Tinta clear colour inks (see project 8). They contain insoluble particles which settle at the bottom of the bottle. Either shake or stir the bottle and pick up ink from the bottom with a wooden or plastic stick. In this way you get a rather dense ink which gives intensely coloured gold lines.

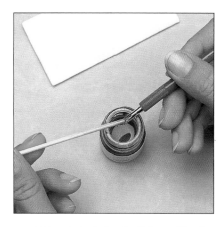

1 Either shake the bottle of Tinta gold well, or open and stir the contents thoroughly with the cocktail stick. Transfer a droplet of gold from the bottom of the bottle onto the nib of the mapping pen.

2 Gently trace over the outlines, keeping the pen almost upright to achieve fine lines. For thicker lines, press a little harder so the nib opens slightly. Do not press at the beginning of a line as this will prevent the ink from starting to flow down the nib. Clean the nib in water and dry it with a cotton rag at regular intervals. In this way the channel of the nib will not become blocked with insoluble or dried up particles. If you have an ink blot, use kitchen paper to absorb most of it, then let it dry and remove the rest with a razor blade or Pergamano eraser.

3 Before stippling, lightly emboss the stippling areas from the back with the large ball tool. You also can use the bottom of the blue handle for soft embossing of a large area. Also emboss parts of the bow. Stippling is done on the reverse side, with the paper lying on cardboard. Use black cardboard or put a piece of dark paper on the cardboard to help you see the stippling. Make little holes by hammering the surface with the 1-needle tool. Hold the tool upright. Stipple the flowers and the flap that closes the bag.

4 This close-up photograph shows the stippled areas in detail. Note how the stippling stays neatly within the outlines and spreads evenly across the area. The holes are so fine that you cannot distinguish them individually. The surface structure of the paper has changed and it has turned matt white.

5 To perforate the outlines, place the parchment paper face up on the perforating pad. Perforate with the 2-needle tool just along the outside of the outlines of the design. To obtain equal distances between the holes, place one needle of the tool in the previously punched hole. You can also use Perga-Soft here; touch the needles on the surface of the Perga-Soft wax and it will smoothen the perforation.

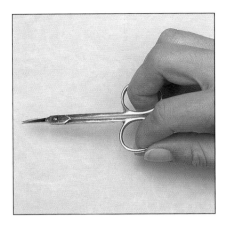

TIPS

• You can sometimes use ordinary scissors to cut out a project. In parchment craft we often perforate a line of holes along the outlines and then cut off the paper with the fine Pergamano scissors. Some people press off the perforated paper with the thumbnail on the soft perforating pad. I do not recommend this as it does not give a fine, regular perforated edge and there is a risk that the paper will not follow the perforation. The best method is to cut the paper between the perforations with the scissors.

• After stippling you can enhance the result by colouring the back of the paper with white pencil.

6 It is important to hold the special scissors correctly. Slide your index finger through one fingerhole and your middle finger through the other. Squeeze one fingerhole between index and thumb. Open and close the scissors by moving your middle finger. The blades should only open 1 mm ($^1/_{16}$ in) wide.

7 Gently insert the blade tips into the holes. Do not press into the holes as this will damage the paper. Note the low angle of the scissors. When making the cutting movement, twist your hand a little to the left.

Hold your work in the left hand at a convenient angle. Repeat in the following holes until the surplus paper falls off. The edges which are not cut in this way are cut using a craft knife.

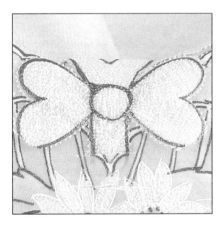

8 Emboss the folding lines on the front or the back depending towards which side the folding will be done. Use the small ball tool and ruler. EF on the pattern means embossing on the front (folding inwards) and EB embossing on the back (folding upwards). Flatten the folds lightly with your fingers, noting the direction of the fold.

Two close-up details of the flowers (above) and the little bow (above right) as they appear in the finished basket. Once you become more proficient at the craft, you will be able to adapt and modify patterns to suit your own needs. For example, the little flowers and

bow here could sit well on a different shaped box or basket. Alternatively, you could use the design on a greetings card or candleshade. This is the joy of parchment craft - its wonderful versatility!

Home Decorations

Parchment craft is not limited to greetings cards, as this spread of items for the home demonstrates. The patterns for the fan, place card, placemat and candleshade all feature a stamped design. Once completed, placemats should be laminated (many copy and print shops offer this service). The oval mount (top right) is perfect for a photograph frame. The flowers here are also made from parchment paper. Patterns appear on page 74-75.

Colouring with Dorso crayons

JAPANESE KIMONO

Parchment paper has a neutral, light grey colour which complements other colours well, making it an ideal material for painting. To change the colour of the paper, paint it on the reverse side with Dorso crayons. The result is a wonderfully soft, diffused tint.

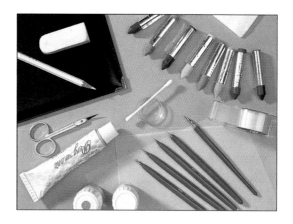

You will need

Parchment paper, size A5 (145 x 215 mm / 5³/₄ x 8 ¹/₂ in)	Lavender or eucalyptus oil
Pattern (see page 70)	Cottonbud
Tinta inks: white 01T and gold 22T	Soft eraser
Mapping pen	Extra fine, small and large ball embossing tools
White pencil	Embossing pad
Dorso crayons, assortment 1	2-needle perforating tool
Thick cardboard	Pergamano scissors
Adhesive tape	15 cm (6 in) pink fabric ribbon, 3 mm (¹/₈ in) wide
Kitchen paper	Pergakit glue

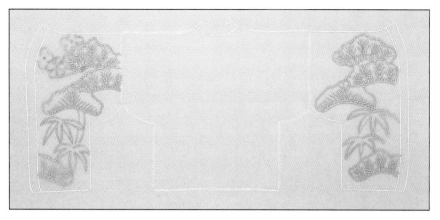

Dorsing is the art of colouring parchment paper with Dorso crayons. After dorsing, the paper can still be painted, perforated and embossed. Dorsing is normally done on the reverse of the paper. The advantages of this are that the colour will be seen through the translucent paper as a smooth and soft tint and the white of the embossing will still be seen as a clear, satin white. If Dorso is applied to the front of the paper, it will cover the white of the embossing. In that case, embossed areas will highlight the Dorso colour.

1 Trace the kimono outline using Tinta white. Use a white pencil to indicate folding lines (after folding you can erase these lines if you wish). Add the gold pattern using Tinta gold and the mapping pen.

2 Apply Dorso red in coarse lines on the back of the paper. It is not necessary to cover the entire area, but do avoid the patterned areas on the front flaps of the kimono. Try not to make sharp lines as it makes the colour more difficult to spread. Go slightly over the outline, except along the lapels and collar.

3 Fix the parchment paper to the cardboard with adhesive tape. This will prevent the parchment paper from slipping. Spread the colour by rubbing with a small pad of kitchen paper. A few drops of lavender or eucalyptus oil on the pad will ease the spreading. Holding the paper firmly, rub vigorously until the colour has been spread evenly.

4 While spreading, some colour may rub onto the lapels, collar or gold decorations on the front flaps and will need to be removed. Clean the gold areas by erasing with a soft eraser. On the lapels use a soft eraser and a ruler for a straight line. The ruler should cover the part where you want the colour to stay.

5 To add the second and third colours to the front flaps, apply a little green and blue (both from assortment 1) behind the gold decorations. Spread the colour with folded kitchen paper or a cottonbud and a drop of oil.

TIPS
• Apply one colour next to another; rub it out and let the two colours fuse into each other.
• If you want a sharp edge, such as the horizon of the sea, cover the sky with white paper, when spreading the colour.
• Keep Dorso crayons at room temperature; cold Dorso is difficult to spread. The warmer the Dorso is, the easier the spreading. If necessary, use a hairdryer to heat the applied Dorso crayon before spreading. In this way the colour will become stronger.

FINISHING
To finish the kimono, emboss the white parts: the collar, lapels, leaves, petals and the white dots. Remember to emboss on the reverse side of the paper. Then perforate along the outlines of the lapels. Fold the front flaps so they just meet in the middle. Perforate along the outer edge of the kimono and cut along the perforations. Make a small bow from the ribbon and glue in place with a dot of Pergakit glue.

To make the picture shown on page 26, make three more kimonos in the same way. Place the kimonos on a soft-coloured mount or make a background paper, including the cherry tree decorations. Display the mount on the wall or fix into a matching frame. The result: a delicate piece of Eastern art.

Colombian flowers

FLORAL GIFT BAG

A parchment project can be embellished with three-dimensional flowers and leaves. Petals made from coloured parchment are cut to shape and assembled to form attractive flowers. Here they are used to decorate a small gift bag. The inventor of these flowers was a Colombian woman, hence the name.

You will need

Parchment paper, size A4 (215 x 290 mm / 8 ¹/₂ x 11 ¹/₂ in)	Perga-Soft
	Pergakit glue
Tinta inks: white 01T, blue 02T, turquoise 05T and leaf green 10T	White pencil
Patterns (see page 71)	Paperclip or cocktail stick
Mapping pen	Tweezers
Dorso crayons, assortment 1	Kitchen paper
Pergamano scissors	Water
Fine stylus and large ball embossing tools	6 pearls, 3 mm (¹/₈ in) diameter
De Luxe embossing pad	100 cm (1 yard) blue ribbon, 3 mm (¹/₈ in) wide

First, make the flowers, then the soft blue bag and let the glue dry before decorating the bag with the flowers. The small flowers have three layers, the large ones four.

Colour a piece of parchment paper 200 x 100 mm (8 x 4 in) with Dorso blue. Blend these colours while rubbing them in. For a stronger colour, dorse the paper on both sides. Trace the

pattern for the petals with Tinta blue. Trace the number of petals indicated on the pattern. Then make the leaves using the green dorsed paper. You are now ready to begin.

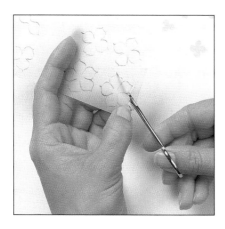

1 Cut out the petals and the leaves with the Pergamano scissors. Cut just inside the drawn outlines as the flowers and leaves look better when the outline is not showing. Always hold the scissors so that the shaped blade tips point away from the petal or leaf.

2 Emboss the petals on the embossing mat with the large embossing tool until the edges curl up in a realistic way. Keep them steady by holding them with your index finger.

3 Carefully emboss the veins of the leaves on the embossing mat using the fine stylus tool. This will create a very realistic effect.

4 Take a dab of Pergakit glue from the tube with a cocktail stick. Glue the largest petal and the next size on top of each other. The petals should be at an angle, rather than sitting directly on top of each other. Use tweezers to hold the petals. Assemble all the flowers in this way. Close the Pergakit tube tightly to prevent the glue drying out.

5 As a finishing touch, carefully glue a pearl bead in the centre of each flower. Hold the pearl with the tweezers and use a cocktail stick to add a small dab of glue.

6 To make the bag, trace the outline with a white pencil and dorse the paper with Dorso blue. Cut out the bag with paper scissors or use a craft knife and ruler. Emboss the folding lines (note: EB means emboss on the back, EF emboss on the front). Make incisions where indicated and fold the top part inwards. Punch the two holes with a leather puncher or a paper perforator or perforate around the hole and cut it out. Fold the bag together, flattening the folds so that the box will adopt its shape without being glued.

Then unfold the bag and glue the flowers and leaves in position. Use a cocktail stick or large paperclip for transferring the Pergakit onto the spot. Leave to dry for one hour. Finish the project by assembling the bag. Affix the strip with glue or thin double-sided tape. Slip the ribbon through the holes and tie a bow.

TIPS
• If you want a strong green for the leaves, colour the parchment paper with Tinta leaf green 10T. Apply some droplets to a small pad of cotton wool and spread it quickly across the paper.
• When assembling the bag, note that glue does not stick on a greasy surface like dorsed paper, so

remove the colour from a strip with an eraser. You can replace the blue Dorso on the outside of the missing strip.
• The bag is perfect for a pretty feminine gift, such as a silk scarf, pot pourri or sweets. Vary the colour of the bag to match the contents.

GALLERY
Oriental Inspiration

All the projects here were inspired by the designs of the Orient. The kimonos are featured on page 20, the patterns for the other items appear on page 74-75. The chopstick holders make an unusual and novel gift; the cherry blossom takes some time to make, but the results are splendid. The other projects include a fan, greetings card and lightshade (top right) which is wrapped around a tumbler filled with water and a floating candle.

Cutting crosses

CHRISTMAS BELL

Delicate lacy borders are the hallmark of parchment craft, and cutting crosses to achieve this is precise work. Many students have said "No, that's not for me – I don't have the patience". But once they have tried this technique, they find it completely addictive.

You will need

Parchment paper 180 x 297 mm (7 x 12 in)	Extra fine, small and large ball embossing tools
Pattern (see page 71)	Embossing pad
Mapping pen	Perga-Soft
Tinta ink: gold 22T	Pergakit glue
2- and 4-needle perforating tools	Thick cardboard
"Excellent" perforating pad	Water
Pergamano scissors	Kitchen paper
Dorso crayons, assortment 1	

Many projects are decorated with lacy patterns made of perforated and cut-out work. Between the lacework you can emboss small shapes like dots, flower petals, and so on. This you can see here on the Christmas bell.

First trace the flower petals in Tinta white 01T and the rest of the design in Tinta gold 22T. Then dorse the areas which appear coloured in the finished photo. Use a folded piece of kitchen paper to spread the colour accurately within the outlines of the bell. The colours used are Dorso violet underneath the 4-needle perforations, Dorso blue above the 4-needle perforations and Dorso fuchsia for the bow. Remove any excess colour with a soft eraser. You are now ready to begin.

1 Place the parchment paper face up with the pattern in position underneath on the perforating pad. Pierce precisely into the 4-dot combinations on the pattern. Hold the tool vertical. Perforate only 0.5-1 mm deep. Then separate the paper from the pattern.

2 Place the paper face down on the embossing pad. Emboss the decorations in-between the perforations. Use the extra fine tool for the tear shapes and the decorations in the borders; use the fine stylus for the leaves; for the petals and the bow use the small ball tool. Emboss the folding line along a ruler.

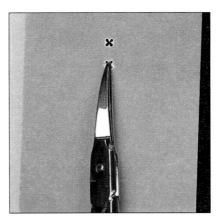

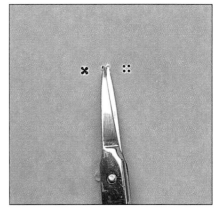

3 Place the paper face up on the perforating pad. Now perforate at full depth by letting the needles slip into the same holes and gently pushing down.

4 The cutting is in four stages. Refer back to project 2 for the correct way to hold the scissors. Put the perforated parchment paper on the black perforating pad for contrast so you can see the perforations well. Hold the paper in your hand at a convenient angle. First insert the blade tips into the two top holes and cut.

5 For the second cut, turn the paper 90 degrees anti-clockwise so the next two holes are now at top. Insert scissors and cut. Do not push the scissors into the holes.

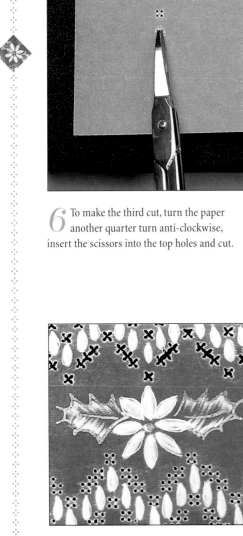

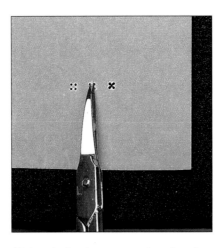

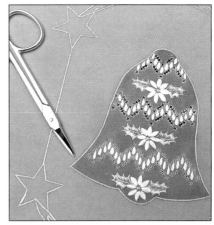

6 To make the third cut, turn the paper another quarter turn anti-clockwise, insert the scissors into the top holes and cut.

7 For the fourth cut, turn again and cut for the last time. With this last cut the tiny piece of paper will fall out. Instead of turning the project after every single cut it is much more efficient to cut first all the top holes, then turn the paper a quarter turn and cut the next row of holes and so on. The turning direction of the paper is not really important. You can turn clockwise if you prefer to.

8 Stipple the four stars. Perforate along the card outline with the 2-needle tool. Crease the card gently at the fold line and along the outlines of the card. Attach the bow with a spot of Pergakit glue, using a paperclip or cocktail stick to transfer the glue. Carefully cut out the card.

This close-up detail of the flower and leaf design in between the lacework shows you clearly how the pattern is created.

 TIPS
• Please note the perforating tools are very sharp. Keep them away from young children.
• The needles might damage your table so protect it with a piece of thick cardboard.

Creative stamping
"STAINED GLASS" CARD

Instead of tracing a pattern, in this project you can use a stamp. This is a very easy technique to master. The translucence of the parchment paper results in a beautiful stained glass effect, enhanced by the window card.

You will need

Parchment paper, size A5 (145 x 215 mm / 5¾ x 8½ in)	1- and 4-needle perforating tools
Pergamano 'Four Hearts' stamp (reference PS4)	Perforating pad
	Small ball embossing tool
Transparent ink pad	Embossing pad
Silver embossing powder	Pergamano scissors
Heating gun or old bread toaster	Water
Perga-Color pen set	White card with a window 66 x 66 mm (2¾ x 2¾ in)
Pergamano sponge on saucer	Paper glue
Synthetic brush no. 2	Thick cardboard

1 Place a piece of parchment paper on the thick cardboard. Wet the stamp on the ink pad and make a print in the centre of the paper. Note the angle of the stamp. Press firmly and do not twist the stamp when lifting it. Avoid getting fingerprints on the paper – hold or touch it only on the edges as the embossing powder tends to stick to grease on the paper.

2 Sprinkle the silver powder over the stamped outline while it is still wet.

3 Tap off the surplus powder onto a sheet of paper and pour the surplus powder back into the container. Small flecks of powder tend to stick to paper where fingers have touched it, so wipe these off.

4 Emboss the powder by melting it. It will become shiny and fixed to the paper. If you do not have a special heating gun, you can hold the paper over an old bread toaster until the powder melts. Do not overheat the paper. You must use an *old* toaster for this as powder may drop inside.

5 Use the Perga-Color pens for colouring. Follow the picture opposite for guidance as to colours. Draw a red line inside the heart outline. Work on one heart at a time so that colour can spread and shade before it dries.

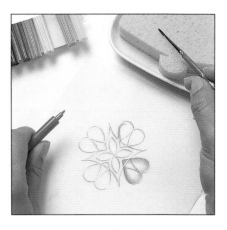

6 Dampen your brush on the wet sponge so that it becomes slightly moist. Spread the colour with the brush by making small circular movements. This pushes the colour towards the outline but also shades it inwards.

7 Always clean the brush if you change colour, dry it and wet it again on the sponge. It is handy to hold the Perga-Color and the brush at the same time. Colour the central part of the design blue in the same way.

8 To finish the design, stipple the large white cross. Mark the corner perforations with the 4-needle tool. Emboss the dots. Perforate for the second time. Cut the crosses. Perforate the 8 small cut-outs with the 2-needle tool. Cut out these spaces.

To cut the paper to size, centre the design in the window by laying the card over the parchment paper. Mark the four corners of the cut-out card on the paper. You can do this by piercing holes at the corners or by marking the corners with a pen. Cut along these holes.

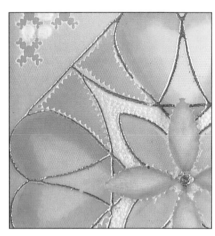

FINISHING

If you want to cover the back of the parchment paper with a paper in the same colour as the cut-out card, cut the artwork 1 cm ($^3/_8$ in) smaller on all sides. This will still allow space to fix it with glue or double-sided tape behind the aperture. For a backlit effect, cut a corresponding opening in the cover and stand the open card where it will catch light from behind. If you wish, decorate the front of the card with a greeting in Tinta gold or silver using calligraphic handwriting.

 TIPS

• If necessary, use the tracing pen and Tinta silver to touch up parts of the print where the printing and embossing step did not work properly.
• To avoid grease on the parchment paper, put a tissue or a sheet of paper underneath your hand while working.

PROJECT SEVEN

Advanced stamping

TIFFANY-STYLE CANDLESHADE

Make your own Tiffany shade by using this tulip stamp. The soft glow of the nightlight provides a soft background light, allowing the painted decorations on the translucent shade to be seen at their best. A shade of this size sits neatly on top of a wine glass, with a nightlight tucked inside.

You will need

Parchment paper, size A4 (215 x 290 mm / 8¹⁄₂ x 11¹⁄₂ in)	1- and 4-needle perforating tools
Pattern (see page 71)	Perforating pad
Pergamano 'Creative tulip' stamp (reference PS6)	Small ball embossing tool
	Embossing pad
Pergamano stamping ruler	Pergamano scissors
Transparent ink pad	Water
Silver embossing powder	Ruler
Heating gun or an old bread toaster	Thin double-sided tape
Perga-Color pen set	Thick cardboard
Pergamano sponge on a saucer	Wine glass
Synthetic brush no. 2	Nightlight

The black dots on the pattern indicate the exact position of the tulip stamp. First, make a template to help you decide the position of the stamp. Cut a piece of parchment paper 10 x 10 cm (4 x 4 in) with one corner that is exactly 90 degrees. Mark this corner with a cross. Place the stamping ruler tight against that corner. Also mark the stamp with a cross in the same corner. You are now ready to begin.

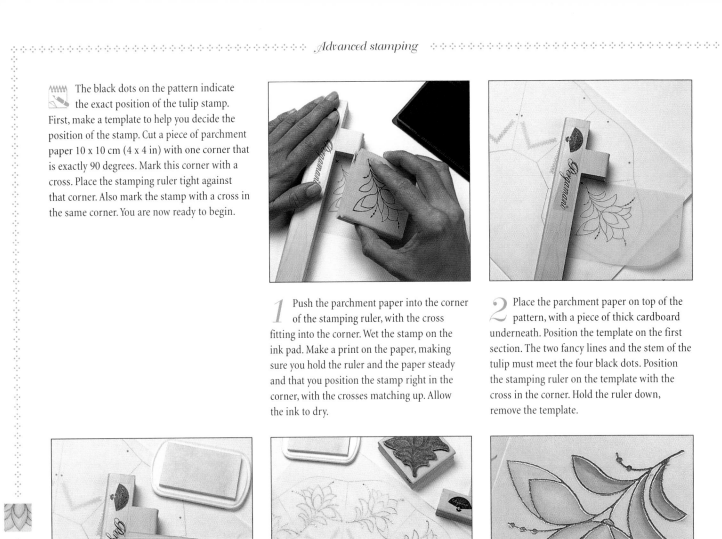

1 Push the parchment paper into the corner of the stamping ruler, with the cross fitting into the corner. Wet the stamp on the ink pad. Make a print on the paper, making sure you hold the ruler and the paper steady and that you position the stamp right in the corner, with the crosses matching up. Allow the ink to dry.

2 Place the parchment paper on top of the pattern, with a piece of thick cardboard underneath. Position the template on the first section. The two fancy lines and the stem of the tulip must meet the four black dots. Position the stamping ruler on the template with the cross in the corner. Hold the ruler down, remove the template.

3 Wet the stamp and make a print in the corner. Once again, the marked cross fits in the corner of the ruler. Make sure the ruler does not move.

4 Sprinkle the embossing powder onto the wet print. Tap off the excess powder and pour back into the pot. Heat the paper carefully until the powder sticks. Repeat with the remaining four segments in the same way.

FINISHING
Paint the tulips with Perga-Color pens. Shade the colours as shown in the finished photograph.

Perforate the fancy lines with the 4-needle tool, using the grid. Do not press too deeply. Separate the paper from the pattern. Emboss between the perforations with the small ball tool. Perforate again, this time pressing deeply. Cut the perforations with the Pergamano scissors.

To finish, cut along the bottom edges with normal scissors. Perforate the top edge with the 4-needle tool. Emboss the fold lines on the back. Carefully fold the shade and secure with double-sided tape along the join. The shade is now ready to place on a wine glass and can be used over and over again.

TIPS
• This shade is perfectly safe to use with a nightlight and wine glass. However, never leave a burning nightlight unattended.
• Pour a drop of water into the glass to keep it cool. The nightlight will float on the water.
• Use black ink to make the template. It shows up well and will help precise positioning.

Colouring with Tinta inks

FLORAL ENVELOPE

The soft grey of parchment provides the perfect foil for the muted colours of Tinta inks. These inks are used for tracing patterns and also for painting with a brush. Good shading effects can be made by playing with the density of colour. This project demonstrates striping – an easy way to get started with these particular inks.

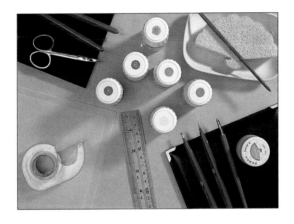

You will need

Parchment paper, size A4 (215 x 290 mm / 8$^1/_2$ x 11$^1/_2$ in)	Small and large ball embossing tools
Pattern (see page 72)	Perga-Soft
Tinta inks: blue 02T, red 03T, light green 04T, violet 07T, leaf green 10T, yellow 16T and gold 22T	Embossing pad
	Pergamano scissors
Mapping pen	Ruler
Paintbrush no. 2	Water
2- and 4-needle perforating tools	Sponge
	Kitchen paper
Perforating pad	Adhesive tape

Instead of painting with a brush you can "colour" with the mapping pen by making stripes. Thinner lines make the effect of striping look softer. Larger distances also make the colouring softer, but the pale grey colour of the parchment paper between the stripes makes the colour look lighter and more of a pastel shade. Look at the picture and see where the lines stop and start and where white areas remain.

Before starting the project practise on a scrap piece of paper. Trace some pansies and follow the steps. Once you feel confident, then proceed with the project.

1 Begin by tracing the leaves in Tinta green and the outline of the flap and the petals on the flap in Tinta gold. Dip the mapping pen in the Tinta yellow and draw fine lines on one of the pansies. Work on the upper petals, from the outer edge of the petals towards the centre. Do not draw all the way to the centre. Start colouring the lower petals with fine lines of Tinta purple.

2 Build up the colour on the yellow petals by adding fine lines of Tinta red. Build up the colour on the purple petals by adding fine lines of Tinta blue.

3 Colour the leaves with fine lines of Tinta green and Tinta yellow. Colour the pansy buds with fine lines of Tinta purple and Tinta red. By now your picture will be resembling the finished photograph.

4 Add the final detail to the petals with fine lines of black in the centre and give the edges of the petals a stronger, defining line. Add veins and detail to the leaves. Add fine lines to the stems and tendrils with Tinta gold. Make shallow perforations with the 4-needle tool, following the pattern.

This detail of the pansy shows really clearly how the colours are built up. So take your time and practise this technique. You will quickly become accomplished and proud of your work.

FINISHING

To finish the project use the small ball tool to emboss the petals and the dots in the perforation grid; also emboss the folding lines along the ruler. Perforate again, this time more deeply. Fold the envelope and crease along the folds. Unfold the card and make slit perforations. Cut to slits and cut along the outlines with Pergamano scissors. Make the incision for flap to tuck in, then re-fold the envelope.

TIPS

• This delightful envelope is absolutely perfect for a gift of money or store vouchers.
• It is also ideal to accompany a bouquet or posy of flowers.
• As an alternative, make the envelope from a dorsed sheet of parchment paper in the colour of your choice.
• Add an insert of parchment paper or normal coloured paper for your greeting or message.

Painting with Tinta inks

DRESDEN FLOWER CARD

The inspiration for "Dresden Flowers" comes from the world of china painting. It is a technique of painting flower designs on porcelain in beautiful, soft yet vivid colours. Dresden flowers painted with Tinta inks produce an excellent result on parchment. For the best results, you should practise first on a scrap of parchment paper.

You will need

Parchment paper, 180 x 250 mm (7 x 9¾ in)	1- and 4-needle perforating tools
Pattern (see page 72)	Small ball embossing tool
Tinta inks: red 03T, violet 07T, leaf green 10T, sepia 12T and yellow 16T	Perforating and embossing pads
Mapping pen	Perga-Soft
Pintura paint: brown 12, red 03 and violet 07	Pergamano scissors
Brush no. 2	Saucer
Pergamano sponge	Ruler
Dorso crayons, assortment 1	Water
	Kitchen paper

When painting the flowers and the leaves it is important to pay attention to your brush which must be sufficiently moist. The paint here is built up in thin layers. Make sure you do not have too much paint on your brush at any one time and follow the photographs for the correct shading.

Before you start painting the petals of the large flower, prepare two batches of Tinta red ink on your saucer as follows:

Batch A: undiluted, 2 droplets

Batch B: diluted, 2 droplets of undiluted Tinta red and 2 of water

Trace your pattern with fine lines. Use Tinta light green for the leaves; Tinta violet for the small flowers (marguerites) and Tinta red for the large flowers (wild roses). You are now ready to begin.

1 To paint the petals of the wild rose, apply a first coat of Tinta red from batch A in the dark areas. Apply strokes from batch B in the lighter areas. Always paint from outside to inside. Pay attention to the light area and leave it almost white. Allow the paint to dry.

2 Paint the dark petals of the wild rose with batch A. Apply Tinta from batch B to the dark side of the lighter areas to add detail. Allow the paint to dry.

3 Repeat step 2, adding more detail and paying close attention to the shading effects. Allow the paint to dry.

4 To paint the stamens, apply Tinta yellow to the flower centre. Draw fine lines with Pintura violet and add dots at the end of the lines.

5 For the marguerites, paint the petals with Tinta violet, as described in steps 1-3. The veins are shaded with Pintura violet. Paint the flower centre with Tinta yellow and the stamens with Pintura brown. Give all the leaves one coat of undiluted green. Paint soft shades of green on one side of the leaf and then apply detail to the veins.

FINISHING

To finish the card, perforate lightly, following the pattern.

Emboss the light parts of the flower petals very softly with the small ball tool. Do not emboss the leaves. First emboss the fine lines between the dots in the grid with a 1-needle tool along a ruler; work accurately. Emboss the folding line with the small ball tool along a ruler.

Perforate again on the grid with the 4-needle tool. Cut the small and large crosses out carefully.

Place a folded insert of parchment paper inside the card. Here, I dorsed it in light green from assortment 1. Secure this insert in place with two small pieces of double-sided tape, or sew two threads in the fold. Then finish the border by perforating it and cutting it out. Alternatively, use wavy-edged scissors for a decorative finish.

TIP

• Try to take a small amount of paint onto the tip of the brush – just enough for the area to be painted. This is the easiest method of creating a natural shading. The smaller the area, the less Tinta required.

Perforation variations
THREE MAIDS IN A CIRCLE

Parchment craft is characterized by an almost unlimited variety of perforated work and open structure, embellished by white or gold embossing. Here, a beautiful lacy border enhances this painted picture.

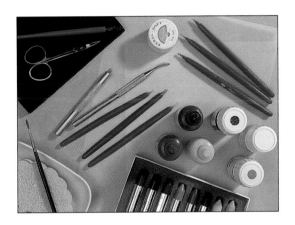

You will need

Parchment paper, size A4 210 x 210 (8¼ x 8¼ in) and 130 x 130 mm (5 x 5 in)	Perforating pad
	Pintura: blue 02, yellow 16, brown 12, bordeaux 51
Tracing pen	
	Perga-Soft
Tinta inks: white 01T, black 11T and gold 22T	
	Dorso crayons, assortment 2
Pattern (see page 72)	
	Pergamano scissors
2-, 3-, 5- and 7-needle and semi-circle perforating tools	
	Paintbrush no. 2
Fine stylus, extra fine, small and hockeystick embossing tools	
	Pergamano sponge
	Water
	Kitchen paper

The painted design and the lacy border are done on separate pieces of paper. The painted circle has a diameter of 115 mm (4 ¹/₄ in) and is finished just underneath the inner circle. Five different perforating tools are used here and each segment of the circular "frame" demonstrates various techniques which result in an array of patterns.

First, trace the design in the circle in Tinta black and the circles and border decorations in Tinta gold. You are now ready to begin.

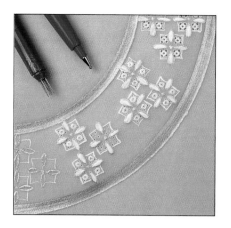

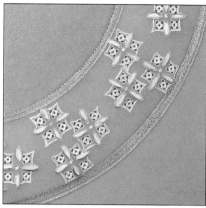

1 Decorate the first sector of the circle with the 5-needle tool. Place the parchment on the perforating pad on the pattern, face up. First perforate gently. Then place the paper face down on the embossing pad. Emboss the fine decorations with the fine stylus. Perforate for a second time more deeply.

2 You can either leave the perforation as it is now or make the shape of the holes oval: when perforating deeply turn the tool slightly to the left and the right. This should be done very softly and gently.

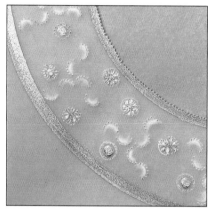

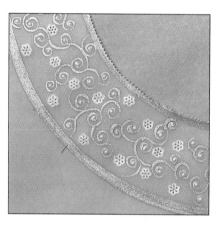

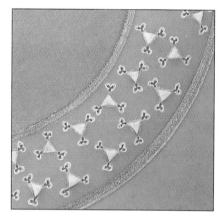

3 Using the semi-circle tool you can perforate semi-circles, circles and scallops or zig-zag perforations. The centre of the perforation is embossed to create a white half-moon shape.

4 The 7-needle tool is called a flower tool as the result looks like a flower (or a star after it has been cut out). Perforate gently, then turn the paper and emboss the decorative lines. Then, perforate the stars deeply.

5 To decorate with a 3-needle tool, perforate gently at first. Turn the paper and emboss the decorations with the fine stylus. Perforate deeply and make the left-right movement as described above with the 5-needle tool. Cut the 3-hole decoration with your scissors into clover-shaped openings.

FINISHING

The central picture of the three maids is painted with Pintura paints. It is not difficult if you trace the pattern accurately and follow the colours listed below. Look closely at the finished photograph opposite to help you achieve the correct shading.

One ribbon is painted with Pintura blue (note the shading), the second ribbon with Pintura bordeaux and the third ribbon with Pintura violet. The dresses are also in Pintura violet. Pintura ochre is used for the hair, the faces are painted with Pintura skin colour.

The picture can then be framed – a circular frame works particularly well. Circular frames are often sold for embroidery, but if you have trouble locating one, contact a framing shop.

Weddings

What better occasion for making a parchment gift than a wedding – and here are just a few beautiful items for you to make. Apart from greetings cards, there are two unusual and exquisite gift boxes, a fan and a lovely novelty parasol to present to the bride. For the dedicated crafter, why not make a bouquet of carnations (right)? If that appears a little ambitious, try your hand at a smaller posy (top left). Patterns are on pages 72 and 76.

Brazilian perforating
VALENTINE CARD

A totally different approach to perforating is to use the metal grid under the parchment. With a special perforator – the Diamond tool – you can create a pattern which is always even, accurate and in straight lines, rather like the weave of linen. This is called the Brazilian perforating technique – it is easy to work and the results are consistently good.

You will need

Parchment paper, size A4 (215 x 290 mm / 8 1/2 x 11 1/2 in)	Perga-Soft
Patterns (see page 72)	1- and 4-needle perforating tools
Tinta inks: white 01T and gold 22T	Hockeystick tool
Easy-Grid template with "Excellent" pad	Adhesive tape, preferably in a dispenser
"Diamond" perforating tool	Dorso crayons, assortment 1
Fine stylus and small ball embossing tool	Paintbrush no. 2
Embossing pad	Pergamano scissors
	Eucalyptus oil

✎ Trace the patterns onto the parchment paper using Tinta white and gold as shown. Dorse the centres of the white outlined hearts and then emboss between the double lines. You are now ready to begin.

1 Place the parchment paper on to the grid, right side up, with the heart you want to perforate facing you and running in line with the grid. Hold the parchment in position on the grid with a little sticky tape.

To align the Diamond tool correctly, place it vertically into the grid alongside the paper. The weight of the tool will help it find its place square on the grid. Lift the tool up, keeping it in the same position to the grid and move over above the first white heart. Always keep the tool vertical and press lightly with an even pressure so that the squares you perforate are of equal size. Perforate into every hole on the grid within the heart-shaped area.

2 After the heart has been perforated, release the paper, move into place for the next heart and repeat steps 1 and 2 until all the alternate hearts are perforated. Remember to use adhesive tape each time to secure the paper and to prevent it from slipping.

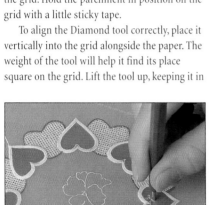

3 Now work on the red hearts, (note that not every hole is perforated – creating a different design). Position the paper first and follow the perforation design as indicated on page 72 (and shown in closer detail in the picture below).

4 When the perforation is complete, apply white lines in a criss-cross pattern as shown in the detail using no. 2 brush and Tinta white.

5 Using the 4-needle tool, and starting on the line that leads from the fold into the heart circle, perforate around the entire outline. Let two needles glide into the former holes so that all the perforations are equally spaced. Finish by perforating along the second line which leads back to the fold of the card.

The Brazilian perforation technique in detail shows the two variations of pattern used on this card.

Painting with Pintura

TRINKET BOX AND BOOKMARK

Painting with the Pintura and Pinta-Perla paints is a joy. It takes a little time to master this technique, but the results are worth the effort. As you practise, you will find that your painting improves every time.

You will need

Parchment paper, size A4 (215 x 290 mm / 8½ x 11½ in)	Small ball and hockeystick embossing tools
Patterns (see page 72-3)	Perga-Soft
Pintura paints: yellow 16, green 08 and bordeaux 51	Embossing pad
	Perforating pad
Pinta-Perla paints: yellow 16N and fuchsia 20N	Pergamano scissors
Paintbrush no. 2	Pergamano sponge
Saucer	Adhesive tape
1- and 2-needle perforating tools	Kitchen paper

The acrylic-based Pintura gives a soft glossy effect and the Pinta-Perla gives a mother of pearl finish. It is important to paint lightly to achieve a translucent effect, so when embossed the colours will be highlighted by the white of the parchment paper.

Trace the entire design in Tinta white. In this project it is best not to separate the parchment paper and the pattern after the tracing. Keeping the pattern behind the parchment paper will allow you to see the details of the design, such as the veins of the leaves. You are now ready to begin.

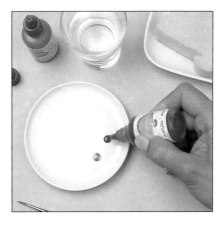

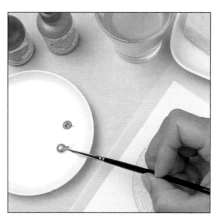

1 First paint the fuchsia flowers. Shake the bottle well to ensure the paint is mixed. Put two droplets of Pinta-Perla fuchsia 20N and two droplets of Pintura bordeaux 51 on the saucer. Do not mix these colours on the saucer; the mixing is done on the brush tip while painting.

2 Wet the brush on the sponge. Pick up a bit of Pinta-Perla fuchsia (not more than 2 mm (⅛ in) on the brush tip) and a tiny bit of Pintura bordeaux at the very tip of the brush.

3 Paint the first petal; start at the petal's outer edge; the tip should point to the outline. Paint with a flat brush and make circular movements.

Point the tip of the brush towards the outline of the petal; turn your paper to achieve this. The brush pushes the colour along the outlines, fading out towards the centre. Paint three flowers in this way.

4 Paint the leaves in the same way – picking up a little Pintura yellow and then dipping the tip of the brush into Pinta-Perla green.

5 The fourth flower is painted with Pinta-Perla yellow and a tiny bit of Pintura yellow. The central rose is painted with Pinta-Perla yellow and a touch of Pintura bordeaux.

The bookmark is painted in the same way as the trinket box pattern, but it is traced first in Tinta black. It is coloured with Pintura yellow, blue, red, ochre, bordeaux and light green. The border is perforated with the Diamond tool on the Easy-Grid.

FINISHING
To finish, emboss the petals and leaves gently. Stipple the border areas around the flowers and leaves, then carefully perforate around the flowers and leaves as indicated on the photograph using the 2-needle tool. These blank areas should then 'pop' out allowing a darker background underneath to show through and enhance your work. Cut around the outer circle with scissors and position in the lid of the trinket box or little frame. The size of the pattern can be enlarged or decreased on a photocopier to suit the size of your box or frame.

TIPS
• Before taking more paint on the brush always clean the brush in water and then remove any excess water by stroking it along the sponge.
• Make sure the paint does not creep up the brush and dry out.

Flower-making

MINIATURE ROSE

Parchment flowers can be so realistic that many people have to look twice before realising they are made by hand. This flower project is a tiny collection of baby rosebuds – perfect for adding to a special gift.

You will need

Parchment paper, size A4
(215 x 290 mm / 8^1/$_2$ x 11^1/$_2$ in)

Pattern (see page 73)

Tinta inks: yellow 16T, leaf green 10T
and sepia 12T

Paintbrush no. 2

De Luxe embossing pad

Large ball embossing tool

Perga-Soft

Pergamano scissors

Glue

Green floral tape

Medium weight florists' stub wire

Florists' reel wire

Mock stamens with large yellow tips

Paperclip

The following instructions make one rose and a stem of three leaves. Make more, as you wish, to create a pretty miniature posy.

Trace the patterns onto the parchment using Tinta yellow for the petals and Tinta leaf green for the bract and leaves. You will need to trace the large petal twice, the small petal twice, the bract once and the leaf three times. Now paint both sides of each piece in the following inks: all the petals in yellow; the leaves in leaf green and sepia and the bract in just leaf green. Cut out each piece with fine or Pergamano scissors. You are now ready to begin.

1 Using your embossing pad and tool, begin embossing on the front of one petal, holding the flower still with the end of the paintbrush. Stroke the petal gently, but firmly, with the tool and gradually, the petal will curve upwards. Repeat this on each petal. Emboss in the same way for the bract. The leaves must be embossed on the back, between the veins.

2 To make the leaves, use the reel wire and cut small pieces, about 6 cm (2 ³/₄ in) in length. Apply glue along the wire a little way and stick to the centre of the leaf. Repeat this process for all the leaves.

3 To make the rose, cut the bobble from the end of the stamen and glue it to the stub wire, pushing it right on to the wire. Cut a length of floral tape in half lengthways and wind it down the length of the stalk. Keep the tape as neat as possible. Using the scissors, make a small hole in the centre of the four petals.

4 Now slip each petal on to the wire, sliding the small petals first. Secure each one with a little glue. Finally, slide the bract in place, also adding a dab of glue to keep it in place.

5 To assemble the rose stems and leaves, start with the rose, wind the floral tape down the stalk, adding in the leaves as you go.

A detailed view of the little rose shows how well it resembles the real thing. Make these tiny posies to decorate gift wrapped packages, cakes, hair ornaments, or as table decorations.

Colouring with pencils – the dry method

ROSE CARD

"Painting" with colour pencils is quite a painterly technique and the fine surface structure of parchment paper allows you to obtain beautiful results. There are two methods: wet and dry. The dry is the easiest technique and this is shown here.

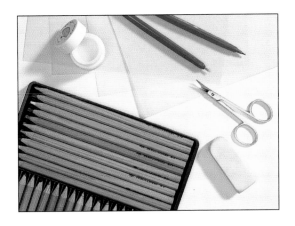

You will need

Parchment paper, size A4
(215 x 290 mm / 8 $\frac{1}{2}$ x 11 $\frac{1}{2}$ in)

Pattern (see page 73)

Tinta inks: green 10T and sepia 12T

Mapping pen

Perga-Liner Combi box no. 1

Dorso crayons

2- and 4-needle perforating tools

Small ball embossing tool

Perga-Soft

Pergamano scissors

Soft eraser

There are two types of pencils for colouring parchment paper: Perga-Liners type A (Aquarel) for water colouring and type B (Basic) for dry colouring and for making a base for watercolouring. Type A pencils are applied with a wet brush and the technique is explained in the next project. In this project you will learn how to colour with Perga-Liner B, or the dry method. The Duo Pencil sharpener has two blades, one for the A-type, giving a thick core and one for the B-type giving a sharp point.

1 Place the parchment paper over the pattern and trace the leaves, stalk and bud in Tinta green and the rose in Tinta sepia.

2 Using the B2 pencil, start to colour the rose and the leaves. Apply the colour softly, filling in the dark areas with fine, short lines. To produce a sharp edge, place your finger at the edge of the design and make pencil strokes away from your finger.

3 Using the B11 pencil, colour the rose by applying red on top of the black and in other areas of the rose. Press slightly harder for a deeper colour. Use the B6 pencil to add dark green on top of the black on the leaves.

4 Use the B10 pencil to add colour to the white areas. Use the B7 pencil to fill in lighter areas and the B6 pencil to add stronger accents along the outlines.

5 To complete the colouring, use the B2, B6 and B7 pencils to colour the stalks and the rosebud.

FINISHING
To finish the card, add a soft shadow of Dorso yellow behind the design, then gently perforate the border. Emboss with the small ball tool between the veins of the leaves, the white parts of the rose and part of the bud. Also emboss the fold line. Perforate again, this time more deeply. Fold the card and perforate along the outlines with the 2-needle tool. Cut along these perforations with the pointed Pergamano scissors to create the decorative edge.

TIPS
• Any excess colour can be removed with a soft eraser. Alternatively, you can use a razor blade if you take great care.
• Adapt the card to a bookmark, a decoration for a memory album or scrapbook, or frame it as a little picture for the wall.

GALLERY
Greetings Cards

Parchment craft is perhaps best known as a means of producing beautiful greetings cards. Here are just a few to whet your appetite. The stained glass effects (far left and below) are produced by a rubber stamp. The other patterns appear on pages 71 and 77 . Don't be frightened to adapt any of the designs to suit your own purposes. The little butterflies shown here, for example, would make super decorations by themselves.

PROJECT FIFTEEN

Painting with pencils – the wet method

ORIENTAL GREETINGS CARD

Watercolour painting on paper is a very popular art. Painting with water-soluble pencils on parchment paper has a lot in common with this. One difference here is that the outline design is provided, so this beautiful card is within the reach of all craftspeople, whatever their level of painting skill.

You will need

Parchment paper, size A4 (215 x 290 mm / 8½ x 11½ in)	Paintbrush no. 2
Pattern (see page 73)	Pergamano sponge on a saucer
Wooden skewers	4-needle perforating tool
Cotton wool	Small ball embossing tool
Perga-Liner Combi Box 1	Perga-Soft
Tinta inks: gold 22T, white 01T and sepia 12T	Pergamano scissors
Mapping pen	Dissolvent liquid or barbecue lighter fuel
Piece of coloured paper	Dorso crayons, assortments 1 and 2
Pencil sharpener	Kitchen paper

First re-read the information in project 14 about the dry method of painting with colour pencils. It is important that you complete that project first.

Parchment paper has a lower water absorption compared to proper watercolour paper. To protect the paper from the water, you must first apply Perga-Liner B type as a base. The base is then spread using a cotton stick with a droplet of barbecue lighter fluid. This makes the parchment paper sufficiently resistant to receive the second layer of colour with the water-based A-type pencil. After that you continue with the Perga-Liners A-type.

Trace the pattern using Tinta gold for the detail in the border. Use Tinta sepia to trace the beak, legs, feet, grass and hills. Trace the sun and the rest of the crane's body with Tinta white. You are now ready to begin.

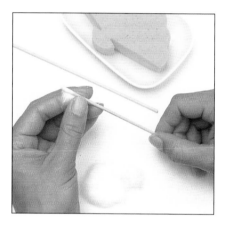

1 Make a cotton stick by dampening the end of a wooden skewer and rolling a strip of cotton wool around the tip. Set this aside until it is required in step 4.

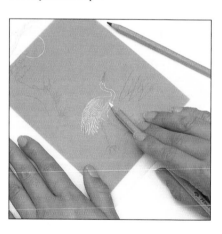

2 Place a piece of coloured paper below the parchment paper for contrast. This will help you to see the traced lines. Using the B1 pencil, draw in the white feathers on the crane's body. Use the B2 pencil to add the black feathers.

3 Gradually build up the rest of the design using the following B-type colours:

Tree trunk: B3, B6   Hills: B3, B9
Leaves: B6   Sea: B4
Crane's legs: B2   Higher cloud: B5
Red part of head: B9   Lower cloud: B4
Neck: B1, B2   Grass: B3, B6, B8
Around the sun: B8

4 Spread these colours to get rid of any sharp edges and to merge the colours subtly. Add a drop of the lighter fuel to the cotton stick.

5 Place the parchment paper on the dark paper to help you see the colours. Gently rub the cotton stick over the pencil to soften it.

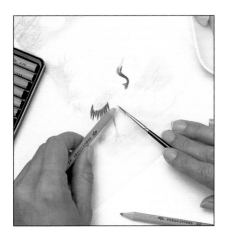

6 Add detail to the picture by using the A-type pencils. These are applied wet. Moisten the tip of the paintbrush on the sponge, then apply colour to the brush from the tip of the pencil. It can take a little time for the pencil core to start to dissolve.

7 The colours used appear below. Note that the sun surround and the clouds do not use the A-type pencils.

Tree trunk: A14, A16, A17   Red part of head: A12
Beak: A20
Leaves: A14, A16, A17   Neck: A1, A3
Crane's legs: A3   Hills: A17, A19
White feathers: A1, A2   Sea: A5
Black feathers: A3   Grass: A16, A17, A19

FINISHING
To finish the card, dorse the background as follows:
Water: Dorso blue (assortment 1)
Around the sun: Dorso orange (assortment 2)
Higher clouds: Dorso fuchsia (assortment 1)
Lower clouds: Dorso lilac (assortment 2)

Place the card back on the pattern and gently perforate the border using the 4-needle tool. Using the small ball tool, emboss the folding line, the legs, some feathers, beak, head, accents in the tree trunk, and dots and ornaments in the border. Perforate again, this time deeply, and cut the perforations to crosses. Fold the card and cut along the three sides with the decorative scissors. Decorate the card's edges with a mixture of Tinta gold and a little Pintura yellow.

PROJECT SIXTEEN

Framing

MEDIEVAL PICTURE

This wonderful picture is a perfect example of the beautiful home decorations you can make with parchment craft. The right mount and frame contribute significantly to its beauty. This project uses many of the techniques you have learnt in the previous projects.

You will need

Parchment paper, size A4 (215 x 290 mm / 8 1/2 x 11 1/2 in)	4-needle perforating tool
Tracing pen	Perforating pad
Pattern (see page 73)	Fine stylus and extra fine embossing tools
Tinta inks: white 01T and gold 22T	Perga-Soft
Perga-Color pens	Pergamano scissors
Sponge	Kitchen paper
Paintbrush no. 2	Frame and mount

This large, and most impressive, project is based on techniques you have learned in the earlier chapters. It may look complicated, but do not be daunted – you can make it! If you can cut one good cross, you can do 100! It is just a matter of patience.

With a large project it is even more important to avoid the sheet of parchment paper becoming dirty. Wash your hands before starting and have a sheet of plain paper underneath your hand.

Unlike the other projects, it has not been necessary to photograph every step. If you are uncertain how to tackle something, refer back to previous projects where embossing or painting were shown in more detail.

Take your time – and good luck!

1 Trace the design using Tinta colours matching the colours of the picture. Paint the design with Perga-Colors using the colour picture opposite as a guide.

2 Perforate gently with the 4-needle tool for the first time, emboss the design partly and emboss the black ornaments in the perforation area. Then perforate again, this time more deeply.

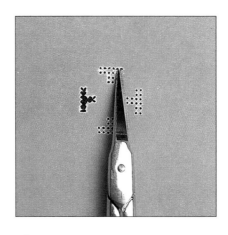 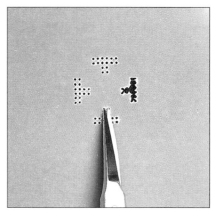

3 Use the Pergamano scissors to cut the t-shaped slits. First cut between the top holes using the scissors. Give the paper a quarter turn and cut between the holes that are now at the top.

4 Give the paper another quarter turn and cut, then turn again and cut. The tiny piece of t-shaped paper should now drop out.

FINISHING

For this medieval-style picture, we chose a black mount with a gold line and an antique looking gold frame. If you wish, put glass in the frame to protect the work against dust and damage. Frames and mounts often have to be made especially for pictures such as this. When you have spent a long time creating a picture, it is worth having it framed professionally, to set it off to its best advantage.

The whole frame to this beautiful picture is made up of two square patterns. Here, they are shown in detail. By taking your time, you will be able to make a frame to any size you want. This example shows a deep frame

around the medieval-style painting: a design which is very much in keeping with the style. However, there is no reason why you cannot make a narrower frame for another picture or photograph of your choice.

GALLERY
Celebrations

For a special celebration, such as a graduation or a new baby, there is nothing quite like a parchment craft memento. Here, we have included a range of projects. Christmas bells, father's day shirts and ties, baby bootees, graduation scroll, mother's day card (bottom right) and a delightful little clown gift box for a child's birthday party. The patterns all appear on page 77-78.

Templates

On the following pages you will find templates for all the patterns used in this book. To enlarge them to their correct size, you must photocopy them at 200 per cent. On patterns which need to be square (gift boxes, etc) please check the final result with a set square just in case the copier has slightly distorted the image.

Project 1: Water Lily Card, page 10

Practise strokes for Project 1

a) large ball (3 mm)
b) small ball (1.5 mm)
c) extra fine ball (1 mm)
d) fine stylus
e) hockey stick tool

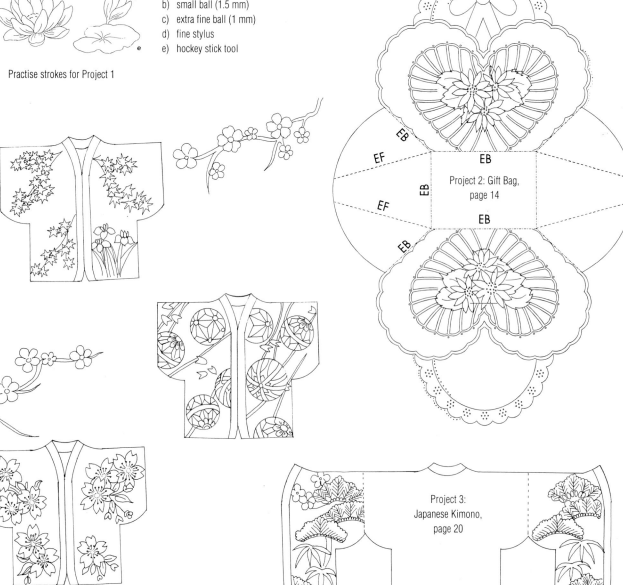

Project 2: Gift Bag, page 14

Project 3: Japanese Kimono, page 20

Gallery: Oriental Inspiration, page 26

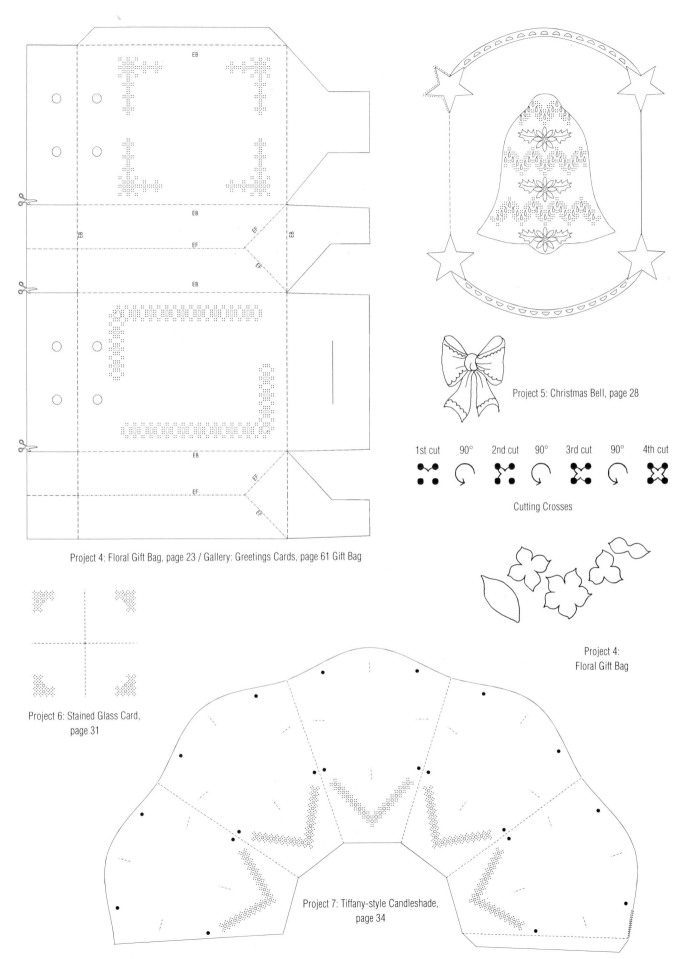

Project 4: Floral Gift Bag, page 23 / Gallery: Greetings Cards, page 61 Gift Bag

Project 5: Christmas Bell, page 28

1st cut	90°	2nd cut	90°	3rd cut	90°	4th cut

Cutting Crosses

Project 4:
Floral Gift Bag

Project 6: Stained Glass Card,
page 31

Project 7: Tiffany-style Candleshade,
page 34

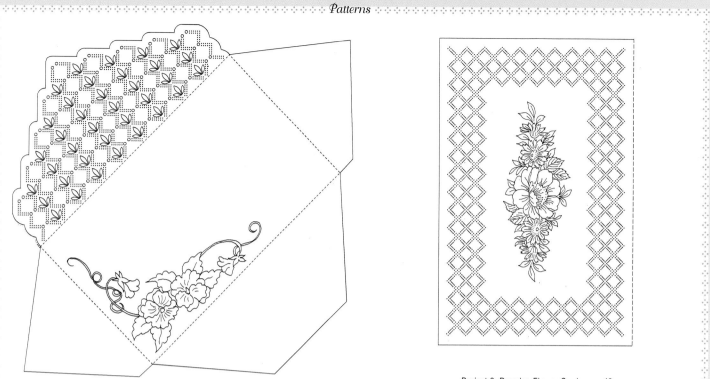

Project 8: Floral Envelope, page 37

Project 9: Dresden Flower Card, page 40

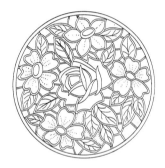

Project 12: Trinket Box, page 51

Gallery: Weddings, page 47 Carnations

Project 10: Three Maids in a Circle, page 43

Project 11: Valentine Card, page 48

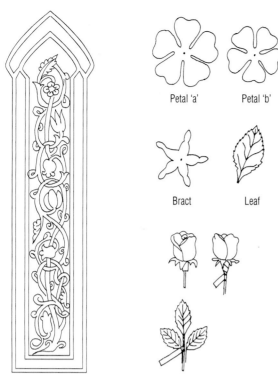

Petal 'a'   Petal 'b'

Bract   Leaf

Project 12: Bookmark, page 51   Project 13: Miniature Rose, page 54

Project 15: Oriental Greetings Card, page 62

Project 14: Rose Card, page 57

Project 16: Medieval Picture, page 65

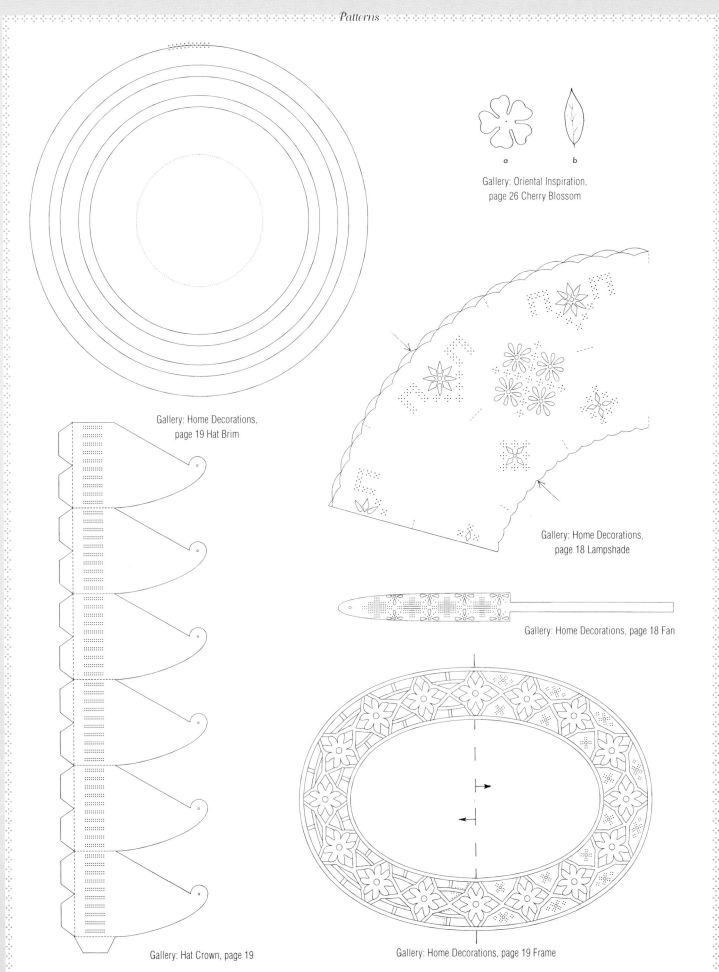

Gallery: Oriental Inspiration,
page 26 Cherry Blossom

Gallery: Home Decorations,
page 19 Hat Brim

Gallery: Home Decorations,
page 18 Lampshade

Gallery: Home Decorations, page 18 Fan

Gallery: Hat Crown, page 19

Gallery: Home Decorations, page 19 Frame

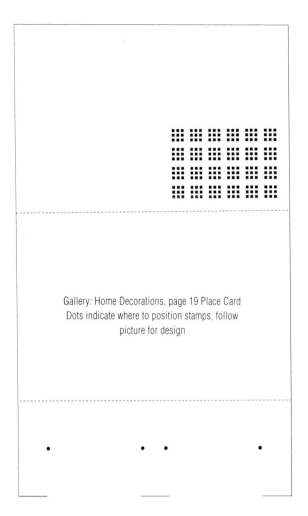

Gallery: Home Decorations, page 19 Place Card
Dots indicate where to position stamps, follow
picture for design

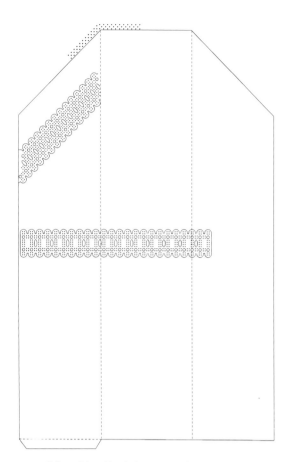

Gallery: Oriental Inspiration, page 27 Chopstick Holder

Border pattern shown on the
front cover of this book

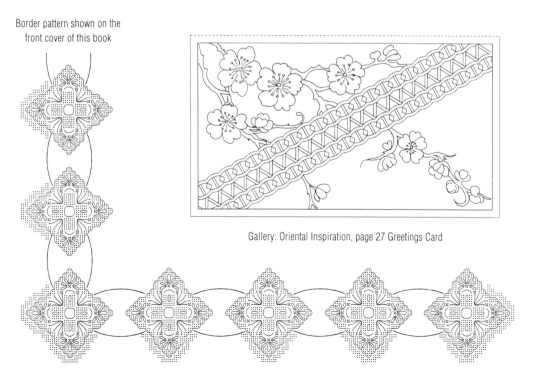

Gallery: Oriental Inspiration, page 27 Greetings Card

Gallery: Oriental Inspiration,
page 26 Fan

Gallery: Weddings, page 46 Parasol

Gallery: Weddings, page 46 Gift Box

Gallery: Weddings, page 46 Posy

Gallery: Weddings, page 46-47 Greetings Cards

Copy pattern, turn paper over and trace the right half with pencil on back. Copy at front with white ink, erase pencil lines at back.

Gallery: Weddings, page 46 Gift Box (base)

Gallery: Greetings Cards, page 60

Gallery: Greetings Cards, page 60

Gallery: Celebrations, page 68
Father's Day Card

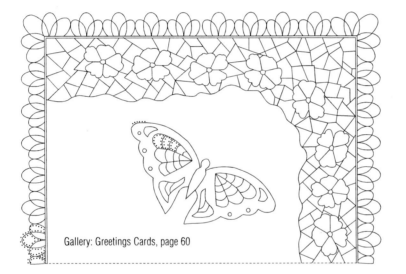

Gallery: Greetings Cards, page 60

BCD
EFG
HIJ
KLM
NOP
QRS
TUV
WX
YZ

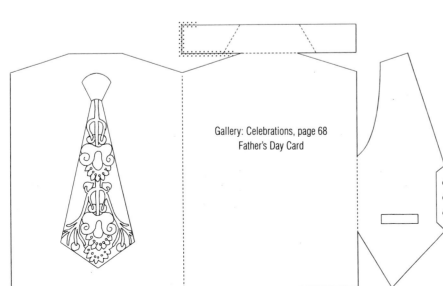

Gallery: Celebrations, page 68
Father's Day Card

Alphabet for Father's Day
card, page 68

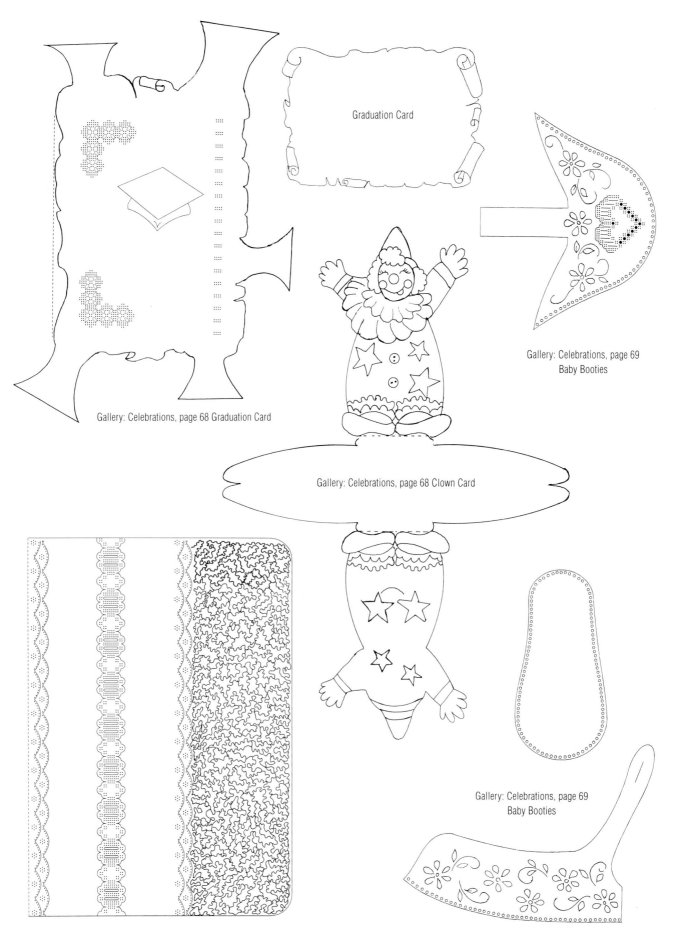

Graduation Card

Gallery: Celebrations, page 68 Graduation Card

Gallery: Celebrations, page 69
Baby Booties

Gallery: Celebrations, page 68 Clown Card

Gallery: Celebrations, page 69
Baby Booties

Gallery: Celebrations, page 69 Rose Card

Suppliers and Further Information

PERGAMANO MATERIALS
A catalogue with full details of the Pergamano materials for parchment craft plus many project ideas can be obtained from your local Pergamano stockist (see below).

OTHER PERGAMANO INSTRUCTION BOOKS BY MARTHA OSPINA

Pergamano: Basic Techniques (tracing, embossing, perforating, cutting, dorsing, stippling)

Pergamano: Painting on Parchment

Pergamano: Beautiful Pastel Cards (colouring with Perga-Liners)

Pergamano: Stamping on Parchment

All books published by LRV Kreatief, The Netherlands. A 45-minute general instruction video in English is also available.

QUALIFIED PERGAMANO TUTORS
Pergamano tutors are available in a number of countries. They have been trained by the Pergamano head office in The Netherlands. Contact your local office for details.

PERGAMANO EVENTS
In some countries, Pergamano events are held for the public, with demonstrations, exhibitions and workshops. Contact your local office for details.

PERGAMANO WORLD MAGAZINE
This magazine contains patterns with instructions and colour photographs of the finished pieces, news about techniques and materials and information on how to use them, further information about events, readers' letters and tips, a pen pal page, etc.

PERGAMANO STOCKISTS
Information about stockists in your area can obtained from the companies listed below:

AUSTRALIA:
Rossdale PTY Ltd
P.O. Box 222
Abbotsford
Victoria 3067
Tel: 03 9482 3988
Fax: 03 9482 3874

BENELUX:
Marjo-Arte B.V.
P.O. Box 2288
1180 EG Amstelveen
The Netherlands
Tel: 020 641 00 54
Fax: 020 645 41 81
E-mail: Info@Pergamano.com
Site: www.pergamano.com

CANADA:
Ecstasy Crafts
630 Shannonville Rd
Shannonville, Ontario
KOK 3AO
Tel: 613 968 4271
Fax: 613 968 7876
E-mail: info@ecstasycrafts.com
Site: www.ecstasycrafts.com

DENMARK:
Fredensborg Indkopscentral A/S
Hojvangen 10
3480 Fredensborg
Tel: 48 47 55 22
Fax: 48 48 44 53 / 51 44

DENMARK:
Stenboden Skjern A/S
Svinget 22
6900 Skjern
Tel: 97 35 17 22
Fax: 97 35 06 01

JAPAN:
CEO Corp.
Rune Fujinomori 502
92-1 Mukaihatacyo Fukakusa
Fushimi-Ku, Kyoto 612-0861
Tel/Fax: 075 645 4051

NEW ZEALAND:
R & R Pocock Ltd
C/- Otonga Road Post Centre
Private Bag 3048
Rotorua
Tel: 07 348 5505
Fax: 07 348 9499

SINGAPORE:
Art of Crafts
02-10 Orchard Point
160 Orchard Road
Singapore 238842
Tel: 235 6267
Fax: 235 9039

SOUTH AFRICA:
Perga Kuns SA
P.O. Box 3199
Kenmare 1745
Tel: 011 665 2009
Fax: 011 660 1934

UK:
Pergamano Ltd
Curzon Road
Sudbury
Suffolk CO10 6XW
Tel: 01787 882330
Fax: 01787 310179

USA:
Ecstasy Crafts
PO BOX 525
Watertown,
NY 13601
Tel: 613 968 4271
Fax: 613 968 7876
Site: www.ecstasycrafts.com

If your country is not listed, please contact the Pergamano head office in the Netherlands:
Marjo-Arte B.V.
P.O. Box 2288
1180 EG Amstelveen
The Netherlands
Fax: +31 (0)20 645 41 81
E-mail: Info@Pergamano.com
Site: www.pergamano.com

Index